Below
the
Green
Pond

Acknowledgments

Executive Editor: Diane Sharpe

Supervising Editor: Stephanie Muller

Design Manager: Sharon Golden

Page Design: Simon Balley Design Associates

Photography: Heather Angel: pages 5 (top), 16-17;
Bruce Coleman: cover (bottom right), pages 6 (both),
7, 11, 12-13, 14-15, 15, 16, 18-19, 22-23, 24-25;
NHPA: pages 5 (center and bottom), 10-11, 20-21, 26;
Oxford Scientific Films: page 9; Science Photo Library:
page 27; Texas Parks and Wildlife: cover (bottom right).

Library of Congress Cataloging-in-Publication Data

Humphrey, Paul, 1952-
    Below the green pond/Paul Humphrey; illustrated by Carolyn Scrace.
      p.   cm. — (Read all about it. Science. Level B)
    Includes index.
    ISBN 0-8114-5739-7 Hardcover
    ISBN 0-8114-3745-0 Softcover
    1. Pond fauna — Juvenile literature.   2. Pond plants — Juvenile literature. [1. Pond animals.] I. Scrace, Carolyn, ill. II. Title. III. Series: Read all about it (Austin, Tex.). Science. Level B.
QL146.3.H86 1995
591.909'692—dc20

94-28573
CIP
AC

1 2 3 4 5 6 7 8 9 0 PO 00 99 98 97 96 95 94

Below the Green Pond

Paul Humphrey

Illustrated by

Carolyn Scrace

STECK-VAUGHN
C O M P A N Y
ELEMENTARY · SECONDARY · ADULT · LIBRARY

Let's look at the pond.

That's duckweed. Look! Over there is
a water lily. There's a heron, looking
for fish.

What other animals can you see?

I see ducks and shore birds.

It's fun looking at the surface of the pond,
but what happens underwater is even
more exciting. Let's take a look.

See how they have webs between their toes
to help them move faster?

8

What's that jelly stuff over there?

They are frog eggs.
Can you see the black
dots in the eggs?
Some of them have
already hatched out.
Do you know what those
wiggly things are called?

They're tadpoles.

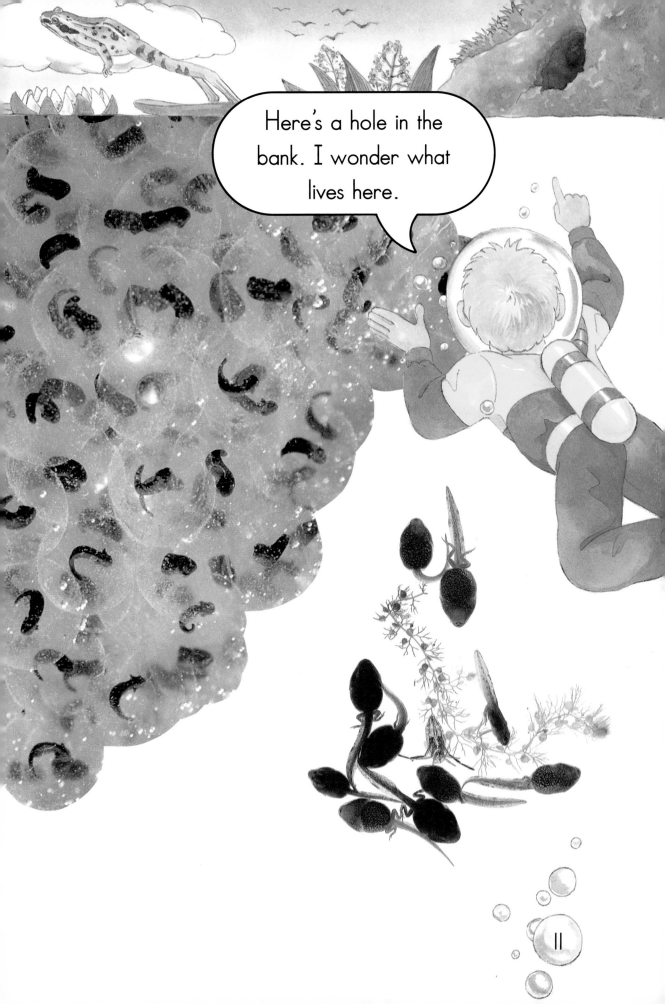

It's a rat. Yuk!

No, it's a muskrat.
It is different from a rat.

13

These animals are great, but some of the smaller ones are even more interesting. Let's shrink down to their size and take a look. But be careful.

Wow! This is scary! Look at that huge fish over there.

14

Pike

Trout

It's not really huge. It's just that you are small. Now you know what it is like to be as tiny as an insect.

16

No, those are the eggs of the greater pond snail. The shell of the greater pond snail can be up to two inches long.

Look! What is happening here?

This spiny male stickleback has made a nest. Now he is "dancing" to attract a female. She will lay her eggs in the nest, but then the male looks after them.

They make him look
handsome to a female.

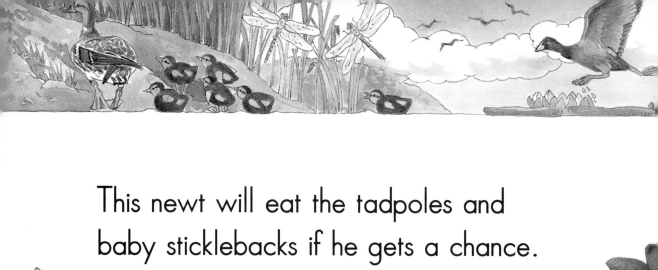

This newt will eat the tadpoles and baby sticklebacks if he gets a chance.

Look at his spines.
He looks like a stegosaurus.

23

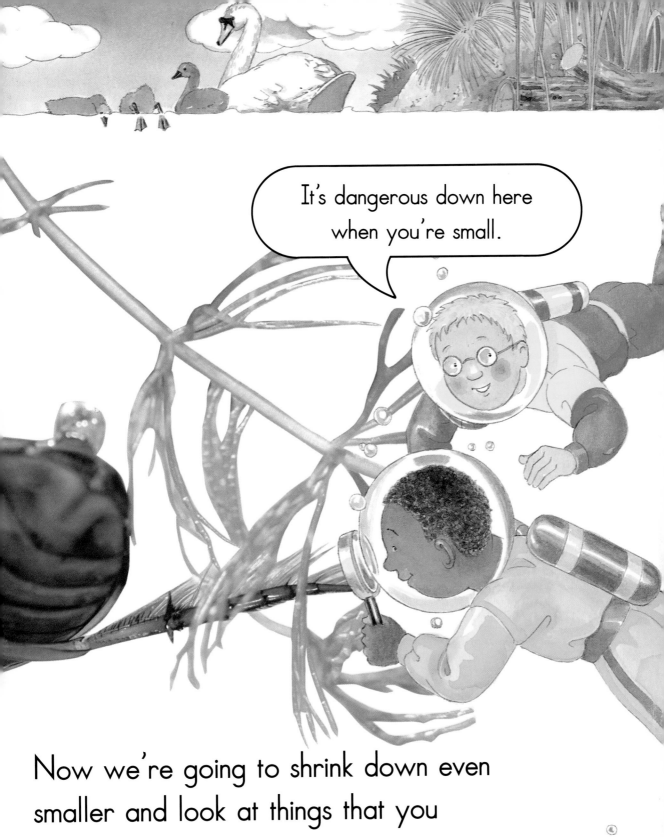

Now we're going to shrink down even smaller and look at things that you can't usually see.

They are Cyclops and Daphnia. They are
so small that you need a magnifying glass to
see them.

Look at the picture. How many of the
animals and plants can you name?
The answers are on the last page, but don't
look until you have tried naming everything.

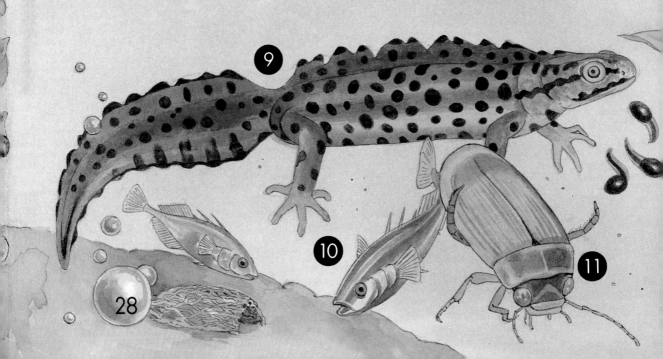

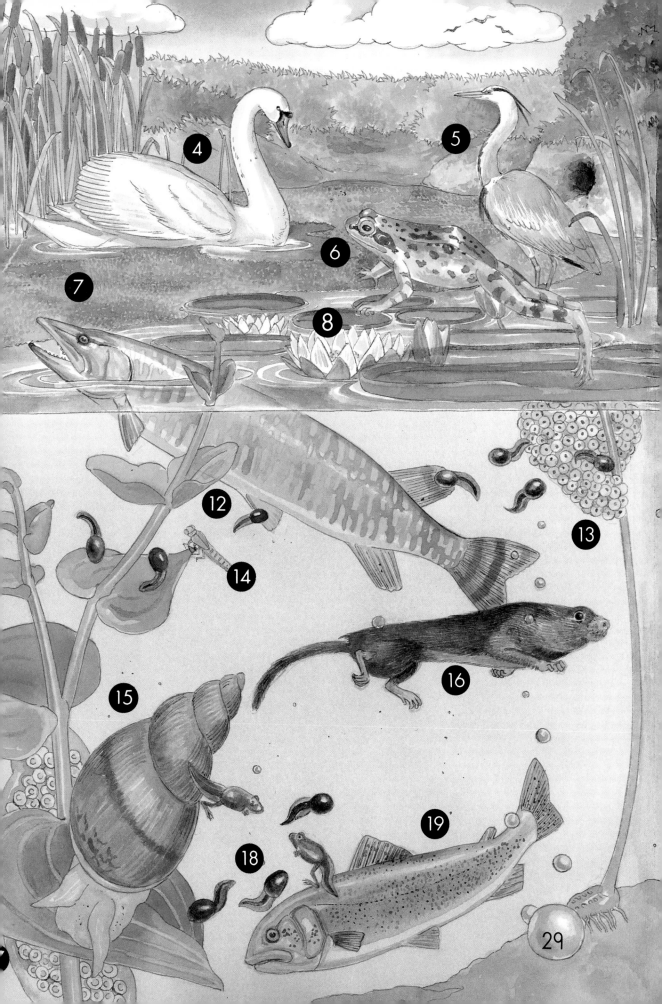

The photographs in this book show many animals much bigger than their real sizes. Below you can see how big the animals really are compared to you.

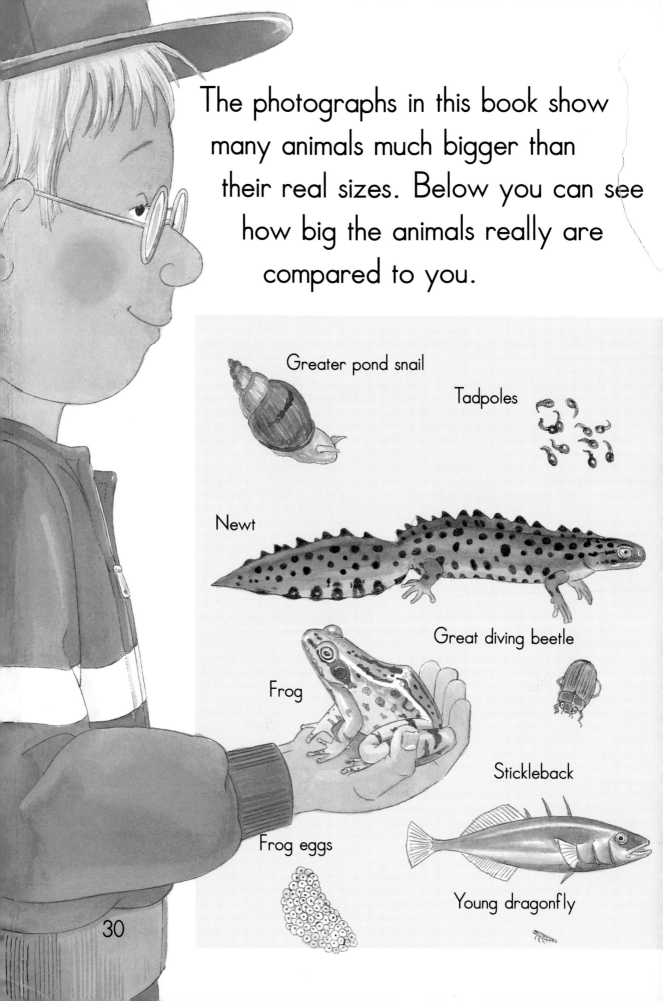

Greater pond snail

Tadpoles

Newt

Frog

Great diving beetle

Stickleback

Frog eggs

Young dragonfly

Heron

Duck

Shore bird

Muskrat

Trout

Pike

Swan

Index

31

Answers: 1. Dragonfly 2. Shore bird 3. Duck 4. Swan 5. Heron 6. Frog
7. Duckweed 8. Water lily 9. Newt 10. Sticklebacks 11. Great diving beetle
12. Pike 13. Frog eggs 14. Young dragonfly 15. Greater pond snail 16. Muskrat
17. Snail eggs 18. Tadpoles 19. Trout